Amazing Microscopes

Sabrina Crewe

Illustrated by
Lynda Stevens

CONTENTS

Introduction	4
Magnification	6
Microscopes	8
The human body	12
Microscopes and medicine	14
Fossils	18
Crime detection	20
Plants	22
Household objects	24
Life in water	28
Quiz	30
Glossary and index	31

Can you guess what this photograph shows?

It looks like a monster!

It is a dust mite seen through a microscope. There could be about a million of these in your bed!

Dust mites are so tiny that they are invisible to the human eye. This is what a dust mite would look like if it was 700 times bigger.

Let's find out how a microscope can make things seem so much larger.

A clear piece of glass or plastic can be curved to form a **lens**. Lenses curving outwards are convex lenses. If you look at this girl's eyes through the convex lenses of her glasses, they seem larger than they are. This is called **magnification**.

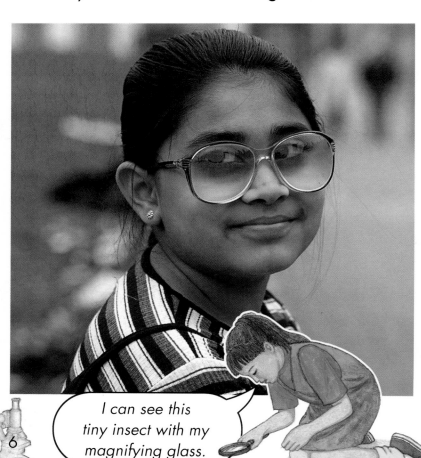

I can see this tiny insect with my magnifying glass.

Magnifying things makes it possible to see them more clearly and understand them better. A stamp collector can use a magnifying glass to learn about the age or quality of a stamp.

The stamps under the magnifying glass appear to be two times larger than they really are. The magnification size is written as x 2.

A microscope is much more powerful than a magnifying glass. Microscopes which use light and lenses are called **optical** microscopes. An optical microscope with more than one lens is called a **compound** microscope.

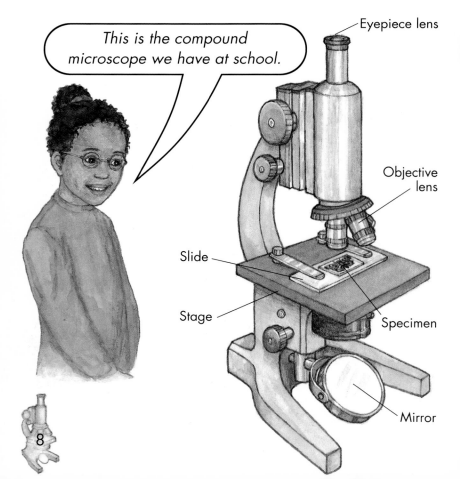

This is the compound microscope we have at school.

Eyepiece lens

Objective lens

Slide

Stage

Specimen

Mirror

To look at a **specimen**, you put it on a glass slide on the stage of the microscope. First the specimen is magnified by the objective lenses, and then it is made even larger by the eyepiece lenses.

When the wing of a tortoiseshell butterfly is magnified 64 times, you can see that it is made of tiny scales.

At x 360, you can see the detail of each scale.

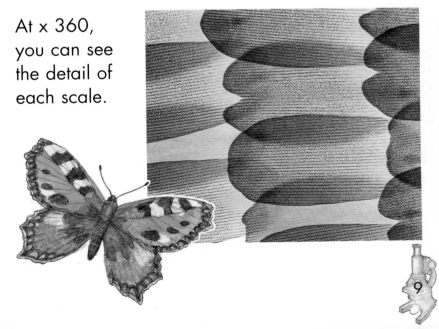

 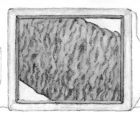 

Electron microscopes use electrons instead of light. They are much more powerful than optical microscopes, and they are able to magnify things many thousands of times.

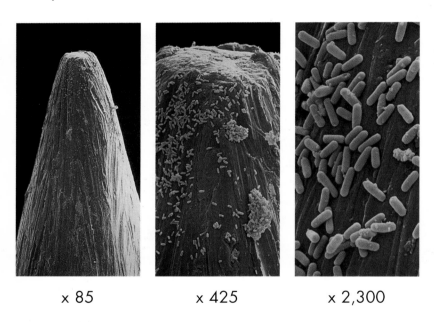

x 85   x 425   x 2,300

This is the point of a household pin, magnified by an electron microscope. The yellow dust in the first picture turns out to be tiny **bacteria** when you look at the pin magnified x 2,300.

An electron microscope makes even the most ordinary things look wonderful. These are some particles found in toothpaste that help to clean your teeth.

x 1,270

Why does the electron microscope have a screen?

Because we do not see electron beams in the same way we see light rays, the image must be made on a **monitor**.

When you look through a powerful microscope, you can see what things are really made of.

I wonder what I'm made of.

x 15,900

All living things are made of **cells**. Every part of a human body consists of millions of cells, like this one. Each cell has its own job to do.

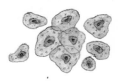

These red blood cells are passing along a blood vessel. The cells travel about fifteen kilometres every day, carrying oxygen all over the body.

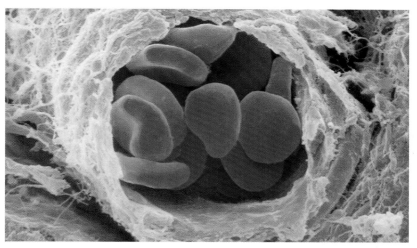

x 2,800

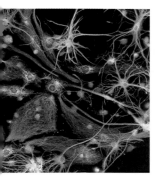

These cells are found in the brain, where their job is to supply the nerve cells with nutrients. The brain's nerve cells send messages to and receive information from all parts of the body.

x 390

Surgeons in hospitals often use microscopes to help them perform operations on tiny parts of the human body. This is called microsurgery.

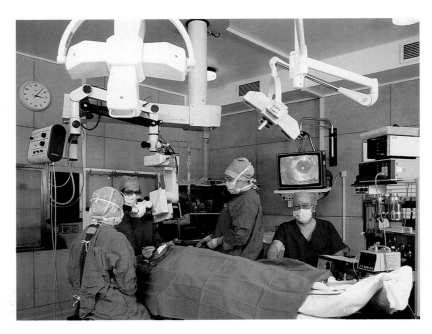

Surgeons operate on a part of a body while looking at its magnified image. On the monitor above the operating table you can see the eye that the surgeons are working on.

One of the most useful things that a microscope can do is to show the cause of illness or disease.

The microscopes in hospital laboratories are in use night and day. Samples from patients are examined to discover what is wrong with them.

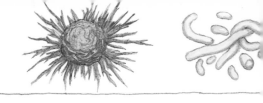

Many diseases are caused by tiny living things called bacteria and **viruses**. This bacterium is called salmonella.

x 25,500

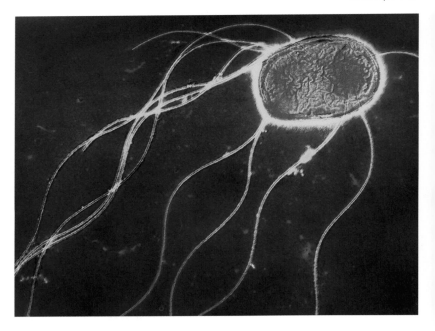

Salmonella bacteria contaminate food such as eggs and chicken. Eating food which contains salmonella can make you very ill. **Antibiotics** can fight the bacteria and make you better.

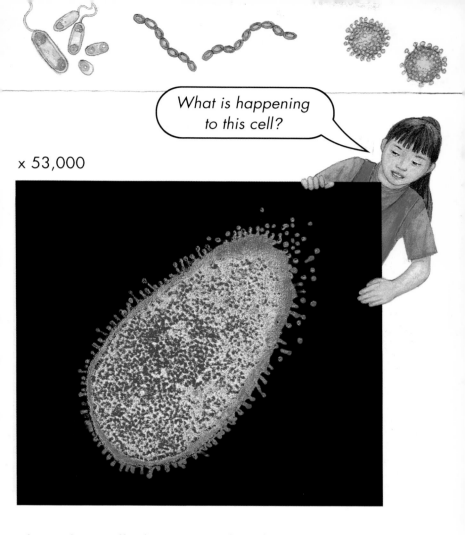

x 53,000

The salmonella bacterium has been attacked by an antibiotic, and the cell is beginning to break up. When bacteria cells are destroyed, the body they have infected can become well again.

Have you ever wondered how we know about things which happened a long time ago? Microscopes can tell us many things about the past.

This looks like an ordinary piece of rock.

The Earth is made from different kinds of rock that have formed over millions of years. Some rocks contain the remains of plants and animals which were buried in sand and mud when they died. When the sand and mud hardened into rock, the embedded fragments became fossils.

You can see that this limestone contains several fossils. These fossils are remnants of **organisms** called nummulites that lived in the sea.

x 18

This rock was formed between 37 and 54 million years ago!

Police detectives use microscopes to help catch criminals. They can examine evidence, such as fingerprints. Everyone's fingerprints are different when you look at them under a microscope.

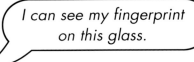

I can see my fingerprint on this glass.

x 6.4

Fingerprints found at the scene of a crime could match those of a suspect. This can prove that the suspect took part in the crime.

With a microscope detectives can examine a tiny fragment of cloth. They can find out what it is made of, and even where it came from.

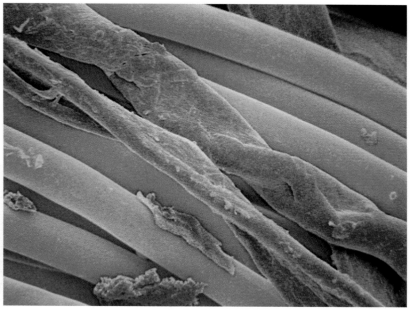

x 1,000

Look at these **fibres** of polyester and cotton. It is easy to match them with similar fibres when they are magnified. A torn scrap of cloth found in a burgled house could match the thief's shirt!

I'd like to see what flowers look like through a microscope.

The surface of a rose petal feels beautifully smooth, but when it is magnified you can see that it consists of closely packed cells.

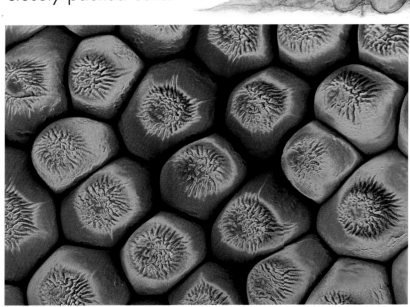

x 1,100

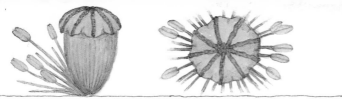

The holes on the surface of this rose leaf are the stomata. They absorb and expire **gases** to help the plant grow. When it is dark, the stomata close up.   x 330

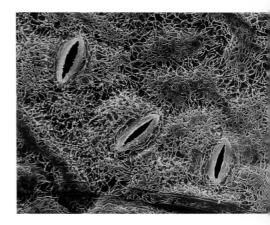

These are grains of pollen from a marigold. Each grain has spikes to grip the body of an insect visiting the flower. The insect carries the pollen to the next flower it visits. The pollen then attaches itself to the new flower and starts **fertilization**.

x 1,100

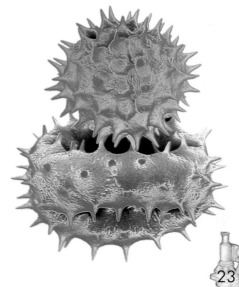

Many things found at home look completely different under a microscope.

Could my pen be magnified?

The tip of a felt-tip pen looks solid when you magnify it 12 times.

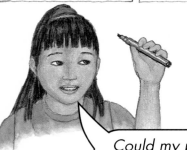

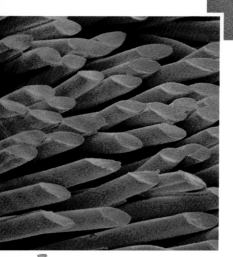

But with a magnification of x 400, you can see that the pen is made from many separate fibres. When you use the pen, the ink stored between the fibres gets squeezed out on to the paper.

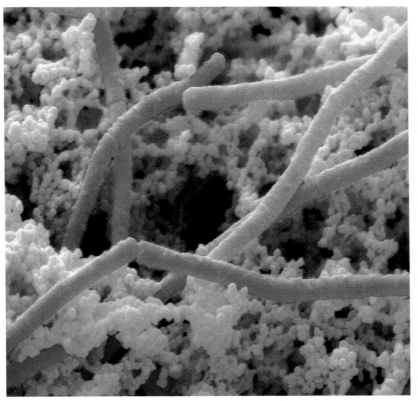

If you magnify live yoghurt 6,000 times, you can see that it contains living bacteria, looking like pink tubes. These bacteria make live yoghurt a healthy food for you to eat.

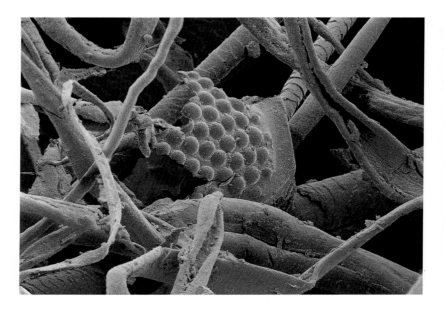

Imagine finding some dust under your bed. What do you think the dust is actually made of?

This is a sample of ordinary household dust, magnified 112 times. The knobbly object in the centre is part of an insect's compound eye! The other pieces are mostly fibres from clothing and furniture, but the grey, scaly rods are strands of hair.

Let's take a closer look at some human hair. A strand of your hair would look similar to this if you magnified it 615 times.

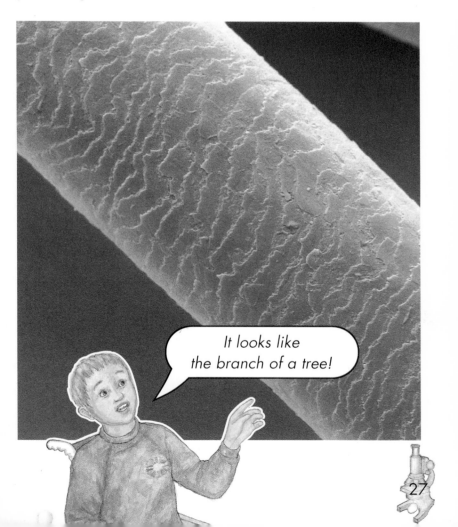

It looks like the branch of a tree!

If you have a microscope at home or at school, you can have great fun magnifying ordinary things.

This water is full of creatures!

x 6

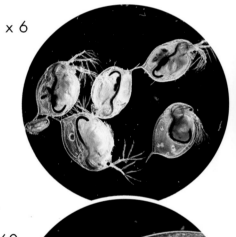

These Daphnia are a kind of water flea that live in ponds. If you look closely, you can see green algae inside the Daphnia.

x 160

Algae are single cell plants that provide food for many water creatures. This alga is called closterium.

Diatoms are an even smaller form of plant life that live in water. These beautiful campylodiscus diatoms would be almost invisible specks if you had them on the end of your finger.

x 513

They are just a tiny part of the world that would never have been discovered without microscopes.

Here are some of the things we have looked at through a microscope. Can you remember what they are? The answers are at the bottom of the page, but don't look until you have tried answering yourself.

1.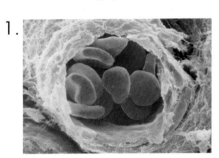

2.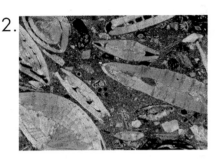

3.

4.

5.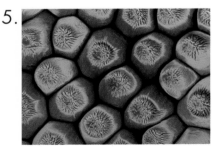

6.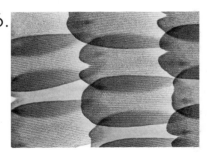

30